JERÓNIMOS ABBEY OF SANTA MARIA

Paulo Pereira

SCALA

M|C
MINISTÉRIO DA CULTURA

ippar
Instituto Português do
Património Arquitectónico

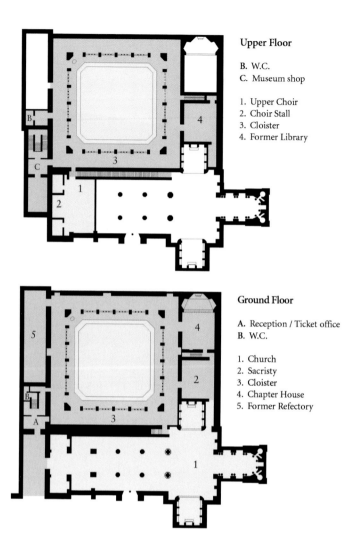

Upper Floor

B. W.C.
C. Museum shop

1. Upper Choir
2. Choir Stall
3. Cloister
4. Former Library

Ground Floor

A. Reception / Ticket office
B. W.C.

1. Church
2. Sacristy
3. Cloister
4. Chapter House
5. Former Refectory

© Instituto Português do Património Arquitectónico (IPPAR) and Scala Publishers 2006

First published in 2006 by Scala Publishers Ltd Northburgh House 10 Northburgh Street London EC1V 0AT

Author: Paulo Pereira
Editorial co-ordination: Manuel Lacerda (DE/IPPAR), Miguel Soromenho (DE/IPPAR), Sandra Pisano (Scala Publishers)

Editorial assistance: Dulce de Freitas Ferraz (DCD/IPPAR), António Ferreira Gomes (DCD/IPPAR)
Picture research and iconography: Dulce de Freitas Ferraz (DCD/IPPAR)
Translated from the Portuguese by Gilla Evans
Design: Anikst Design, London
Printed in Spain

ISBN-10: 1 85759 491 6
ISBN-13: 978 1 85759 491 1

10 9 8 7 6 5 4 3 2 1

All photographs by Luis Pavão, in collaboration with Carlos Sá
Except pages 8, 9, 30 (right), 32 (right), 33, 39: IPPAR/Henrique Ruas; page 7: INAPA/Nicolas Sapieha

Plan: © IPPAR/ Maria João Saldanha

CONTENTS

THE FOUNDATION OF THE MONASTERY

South portal

Restelo, now part of the parish of Belém, was a small medieval waterfront village on the western outskirts of Lisbon, where ships could anchor while their crews came ashore. As it became an increasingly important seaport a chapel was founded there, thought to have been dedicated to Our Lady, Star of the Sea, traditionally the seafarer's protector and guide. Thus the name alluded to both the chapel's link with seafaring as well as to the story of the Three Wise Men who were guided by a star to Bethlehem (Belém in Portuguese). Prince Henry the Navigator (Dom Henrique) gave orders for this small chapel to be extended, dedicating it to Santa Maria de Belém, or Our Lady of the Three Kings, so maintaining the connection with its original patron saint. Administered by monks of the Order of Christ, the chapel's main purpose was to provide spiritual help and support for seafarers. By the late fifteenth century, however, it had fallen into disuse, despite the great symbolic power it had acquired from its association with Vasco da Gama: it was here that the navigator prayed and kept vigil on the eve of the departure of his fleet to India on 7 July 1497.

Strictly speaking, the history of the monastery at Belém only began in 1495,

Aerial view of Jerónimos Abbey

when King Manuel I (1469–1521) asked permission of the Holy See to found a monastery for the Jeronimite Order on the site of the former chapel. Alexander VI granted permission in 1496 in the form of a papal bull. In 1498, as heirs presumptive to the throne of Castile and León, King Manuel and his wife Queen Isabel travelled to Spain to take oaths of allegiance. In the same year, however, the queen became ill and died.

In 1501 or 1502 (the year is uncertain) on the feast of the Epiphany – 6 January – the foundation stone of the new monastery was laid. The Jeronimite monks received further funding in 1503, this time one-twentieth of the taxes levied on goods brought in from India – a much bigger injection of funds than they had previously received. It is at this point that legend and history become intertwined. Indeed, although the foundation of the monastery dates back to before the voyage of Vasco da Gama, it is clear that its actual construction and design came later, since it depended on revenue from trade with India and was a result of the state's wish to commemorate the discovery of a sea route to India.

The laying of the foundation stone on the feast of the Epiphany – the day commemorating the coming of the Three Kings – as well as the choice of patron saint, was an attempt to transform Restelo into a new Bethlehem, a new point of departure for Christianity. The concept was in keeping with the messianic spirit of the Manueline period, represented in the symbolism of the monastery's ornamentation. The unification of the world's Christians, the celebrated search for the kingdom of the mythical Eastern monarch Prester John 'of the Indies', and even the 'miracles' and portents of the period, which were associated with the advent of the second half of the millennium, were all embodied in that symbolism.

Jerónimos Abbey seen from the east, with the Mannerist chancel in the foreground

THE JERONIMITE MONKS

The Order of St Jerome first emerged in Italy in 1377, following on from a religious movement led by Tommasucio da Duccio, originally a member of the Franciscan Third Order. A closed order devoted to prayer, the Jeronimite monks, according to the precepts of their founder, endeavoured to emulate the life of St Jerome, a desert hermit and an important Christian intellectual. In the early days of the Church, St Jerome standardised the text of the New Testament and translated the Old Testament from Greek to Latin between AD 382 and 405.

The Order arrived in Portugal in the fourteenth century but it was during the

South portal

Mosteiro dos Jerónimos, oil on canvas, Filipe Lobo (National Museum of Ancient Art)

reign of King Manuel I (1495–1521) that it became widely established. Apart from his evident devotion to St Jerome (he chose to be accompanied by the saint in the lifelike statue on the west portal) the king's sympathy with the Jeronimite monks lay in the renewed spirituality they embodied. This was in contrast to some other orders whose spirituality integrity was showing signs of debasement and which had, in some cases, lapsed into negligence.

The spirituality of the Jeronimites was, by definition, contemplative, and the monks are believed to have played a significant role in creating a new approach to Christian devotion through promoting the life of Christ as an example and proclaiming the joy to be found in emulating him. This practice was a reformist trend within the Catholic Church. The decorative scheme on the ground floor of the cloister appears to be connected to this fundamental aspect of monastic life. Jeronimite monks also attached great importance to the practice of 'internal' prayer, and the power of the images encouraged a mystical participation in Christ's life and Passion.

THE WORK OF
DIOGO BOITACA

A monument like Jerónimos Abbey is not built in a day. Many factors such as transport delays, modifications of plans, operational problems, changes in taste and, consequently, in architectural decisions, as well as a simple lack of funds, all played their part.

The construction of the abbey is generally considered to have undergone two major phases during the reign of King Manuel I. The first, which began in 1501 or 1502, was under the direction of Diogo Boitaca, a master builder who probably came from the south of France and who had been working in Portugal since the end of the reign of King João II. This phase can be further divided into two periods – before 1513 and from 1514 onwards. The second phase began in 1517

View of the combination of volumes on the upper storey, showing the original cylindrical pilasters designed by Diogo Boitaca, later added to by João de Castilho and Torralva under the supervision of Basque master builder João de Castilho.

There is documentary evidence that the first significant payments towards the project were made in 1502 or 1503. When the king purchased more land for the building in 1513 it was a clear sign of his intention to widen the scope of the project, which already employed some 100 men. From the following year the workforce grew, as did the number of new master builders and ornamental sculptors employed,

View of the lower level gallery of the cloister

culminating in a major review of the construction in 1517.

What was the monastery like at this point? The dormitory block running east to west and the arcades of the porch beneath it must have been near completion. The original chancel was already built and vaulted and the walls of the body of the church would already have reached a great height. The windows and some of the roof supports had begun to be carved and installed, while much progress had been made with the building of the chapels of the transept, and the pillars along the aisles would already have been laid out and planned. However, one of the most critical areas – the vaulted ceiling of the transept crossing and of the entire church nave – remained to be built.

Part of the cloister had also been constructed. The external façades would have had cylindrical buttresses, typical of Boitaca's designs, which were then concealed by subsequent constructions. The south wall of the church had a buttressed portal similar to that of the Convento de Jesus at Setúbal, built by Boitaca ten years earlier. This would have provided a monumental entrance facing the waterfront, as well as adding strength to the wall – which was thinner at this point –, so supporting the internal vaulting. However, it was not Boitaca who would be responsible for the building of the portal of Jerónimos Abbey.

THE WORK OF
JOÃO DE CASTILHO

In April 1516 João de Castilho came on board to work alongside Boitaca before taking over full control of the site on 2 January 1517. After this date Diogo Boitaca's name does not appear on any document, which is probably due to the fact that he fell out of favour with the king following a military blunder.

Around this time the king devised a new set of rules governing the project for Jerónimos Abbey. A papal bull issued on 17 July 1517 named the monastery as the principal house of the Jeronimite Order in Portugal, designed to accommodate 100 monks, a fact which meant that plans would have to be revised. Meanwhile, under the terms of King Manuel's will, drawn up in April of that year, the monastery was to become the royal mausoleum. Significantly the will was drawn up only one month after the death of the king's second wife, Queen Maria, a fact that would certainly have influenced the monarch's decision to make the building an especially magnificent memorial to the late queen.

In 1517, with Castilho now in charge of the site, efforts were redoubled. He co-ordinated work on the first cloister, chapter house, sacristy and side door, managing a workforce of 110 men – French, Flemish,

View inside the refectory
(Filipe Henriques, c.1517)

Spanish and Portuguese – employed on various tasks. The French sculptor Nicolau Chanterêne also arrived on the scene, his high rate of pay reflecting his prestige. Accompanied by eleven craftsmen, most of them French, he set to work on the west portal. Pero Guterres, a Spaniard, worked on the chapter house with a team of twenty-seven of his countrymen. Rodrigo de Pontezilha and four fellow Spaniards concentrated solely on the chapter-house door. Fernando de la Fremosa led a group of ten working on the sacristy. Francisco de Benavente, a Spaniard, led a team of thirty-eight men working on the cloister and probably also on the church. Another Spaniard, Pêro de Trillo, worked with thirty-eight craftsmen on one side of the cloister. Portuguese Felipe Henriques – son of the master builder Mateus Fernandes – and fifty-five workers were assigned to the cloister. A compatriot, Leonardo Vaz and fifteen craftsmen worked on the refectory. João Gonçalves and ten craftsmen tackled three choir chapels, a task they shared with Rodrigo Afonso and his team of ten artisans. The scale and organisation of the building site show clearly that João de Castilho was more than just a master builder; he was very much a contractor in the modern sense of the word, recruiting the workforce, supervising the work and acting as construction engineer. The key to his success was the skill with which he managed subcontractors; sometimes as many as 250 workers were engaged simultaneously on the project.

The work co-ordinated by Castilho led to the completion of the ceiling of the ground floor of the cloister and to the start of the construction of the upper floor of what was to be Portugal's first two-storey vaulted cloister. Despite its apparent complexity,

work on the south portal was completed with extraordinary speed .

Castilho also carried out the intricate task of constructing the ceilings above the nave and transept, to a design that shows both English and Spanish influences, with the ribs arranged in such a way as to produce a 'spiderweb' effect. He left his mark very clearly on Jerónimos Abbey, not only finding solutions to structural problems but also creating a new language for monumental architecture – changing, even transfiguring – its outward appearance. It is almost certain that the work carried out on Jerónimos Abbey under Boitaca was closer to the typical image of Manueline architecture of central Portugal, which was characterised by open spaces, cylindrical structural supports, keel or ogee arches and Moorish or Mudéjar ornamentation. The decorations were hyper-naturalistic, fleshy and elaborately carved. Castilho and the Basque master builders who worked with him introduced a change of style, the architectural ornamentation they used having little in common with the rather coarse naturalism of the early Manueline period. Instead they came to adopt the Spanish Plateresque style – so called because of its resemblance to the art of the silversmith or *platero* – which drew on the classical architecture of ancient Rome. With Jerónimos Abbey as its focal point, the powerful Spanish influences sweeping the architecture of Portugal was, as Rafael Moreira (see bibliography) contends, well suited to the political ambitions of King Manuel, who wished to unite the crowns of the Iberian Peninsula.

THE CLASSICAL STYLE

Political change and sudden ideological shifts naturally had an impact on the monastery's architecture. One of the most important changes came with the succession to the throne of King Manuel's son, King João III. There is little doubt that he lacked interest in continuing his father's project, indeed the new king preferred to concentrate on the Convento de Cristo at Tomar, where he initiated a series of grandiose projects. He adopted a new architectural language, bringing in early Renaissance classicism and concealing and even walling up the Manueline constructions of the choir, which had been completed only a short time before his arrival. He also chose as a burial place

Platband with Renaissance decoration, executed while Diogo de Torralva was master of the works (c. 1540–1551)

Platband in the cloister: Renaissance decoration with suits of armour, busts, triumphs, tondi and mythological figures

the chapel of Nossa Senhora da Conceiçao, a small jewel of Portuguese and Iberian Renaissance architecture, which was close to the Convento de Cristo. This meant abandoning the idea of founding a pantheon for the Beja branch of the Avis dynasty at Jerónimos Abbey, as his father had wished. It was no surprise, therefore, that around 1530 João de Castilho was transferred from the site at Belém (where work ground to a halt) to design and direct the new Tomar building project.

The ideological, cultural and religious philosophy of King João was quite different to that of his predecessor. Initially he was highly sympathetic to the concept of *devotio moderna* (new devotion) and other progressive ways of thinking. Architecture responded to these new ideas by adopting a classical vocabulary 'in the Roman style', which was a radical move away from the late-Gothic models that inspired the Manueline style. As Renaissance was adopted as the officially accepted architectural style it became imperative that this was reflected in what little work was still being carried out at Jerónimos Abbey.

At this point the architect Diogo de Torralva was appointed 'master of the works at Belém', a post he held between 1540 and 1551. His task was to co-ordinate the completion of the various half-built sections of the monastery and to add the finishing touches. He left his mark most clearly on the previously unfinished upper storey of the cloister, where the platband is decorated with busts of imperial-looking figures and a sequence of diamond-shaped tablets containing reliefs of triumphs – festive processions celebrating the victories of Roman generals. He was also responsible for the design of the choir stalls in the upper choir – a beautiful example of the wood-carver's art, exquisitely executed by Diego de Sarça.

More classical touches were added to the monastery by Torralva's successor, Jerónimo de Ruão (1531–1601), who completed the project. Son of the prolific sculptor João de Ruão Jerónimo was appointed master of the works of the monastery in 1563, and worked on various projects there until his death. He is buried in the cloister.

His most important contribution was the reconstruction of the chancel, commissioned in 1563 by Queen Catarina. Begun around 1565 and completed in 1572, it replaced the previous Manueline chancel, which was considered 'small and low'. He followed the vocabulary of his predecessor Diogo de Torralva, possibly even using his design, but his Mannerist approach produced something in marked contrast with the rest of the monastery. Ostentatious Manueline monumentalism gave way to the plain, rectilinear and rigorous austerity of classicism. The theory of Classical Orders imposes a sense of rhythm and harmony, with Corinthian pillars at ground-floor level and Ionic pillars on the upper level. The interplay of black, white and red marble lends an atmosphere of nobility and solemnity to the chancel, which was intended as a family mausoleum. Roofed with a barrel vault topped by a half-dome, the ornamentation is confined to the structural ribs, forming a set of mouldings which frame the panels of the altarpiece on the end wall. Viewed from the outside the chancel stands out from the rest of the construction for its 'hard', solid and opaque appearance, which has resonances of military architecture.

THE 'MANUELINE STYLE' AND REVIVALISM

The hybrid style of architecture that came to be known as Manueline was largely the result of João de Castilho's collaboration with Boitaca and other Portuguese master builders working on projects in Estremadura (in the southern region of Spain) and the south of Portugal. It was an architectural style that would reach its zenith at Jerónimos Abbey.

It is interesting that the term 'Manueline style' was not coined until 300 years later, in a short but influential study of Jerónimos Abbey by Francisco Adolfo Varnhagen entitled *Notícia Histórica e Descriptiva do Mosteiro de Belém* (*Historical and Descriptive Notes on the Monastery of Belém*), published in 1842. In his book Varnhagen compares the monastery with other buildings dating from the reign of Manuel I and finds many features in common. He then goes on to classify them under the heading 'Manueline' – or 'Emmanueline' – architecture. It was usual at this time to view architectural styles as symbols of national identity, as tangible and durable expressions of the spirit of a people. In this way Varnhagen credited the Portuguese people with their own national style, the high point of which coincided with the reign of Manuel I and with the glorious days of maritime discovery and the expansion of the empire. The term 'Manueline architecture' quickly became common currency among the intelligentsia of the period.

The concept also appealed to more radical Romantic nationalists such as the French historian Edgar Quinet. In 1857 he wrote enthusiastically about the building, extolling its iconographic features as references to the sea and seafaring. This distorted interpretation of the architecture of the Manueline period, fed by its associations with the great voyages of discovery, became widespread in the nineteenth century and was adopted by travellers and the educated classes. For better or worse the Manueline style came to be associated with the maritime and the exotic. We now know that the maritime symbols such as ropes, fish, anchors and ships are in parts of the building that were restored at various times. The nineteenth-century restorers accepted the notion that the Manueline style represented Portugal's maritime history and went on to perpetuate the myth with their own exaggerations and anachronisms.

In 1807 the country was immersed in civil war and Jerónimos Abbey was occupied by troops. When the religious orders were abolished by decree on 28 December 1833 the monastery was abandoned until it was given over to the charitable organisation, the Casa Pia. Twenty-six years later, disturbed by the dilapidated state into which the building had fallen, and the poor conditions in which the charity that occupied it was having to work, the head of the Casa Pia, Eugénio de Almeida, proposed that work be undertaken to adapt the monastery to suit the needs of charity workers and those in their care. The Ministry of Public Works then decided to launch a major rebuilding programme to enable the charity to operate in a dignified manner, an initiative that also had the support of King Fernando II.

A number of engineers and architects produced studies and designs for the restoration, among them French architect J. Colson (from 1859 to 1861), Valentim José Correia (from 1863 to 1865) and English architect Samuel Bennett (from 1865 to 1867). None succeeded in bringing their plans to fruition and the Italian set designers Aquiles Rambois and Giuseppe Cinatti, from Lisbon's Teatro de São Carlos, eventually took the reins. They embarked on

Detail of one of the cloister arches:
a ship, probably carved in the
18th century during restoration

a project (1867–78) to remodel and restore the dormitory building, making it more symmetrical. Following the same principles they added a finishing touch to the west end in the form of a 'formal' façade. Of all the subsequent additions the most absurd was the Indian-style dome shaped like a bishop's mitre built on top of the church's choir; it replaced the former pyramidal bell-tower. In the middle of the building that ran parallel to the river, the set designers proposed to build a three-sided tower with four pinnacles, a part of the project that was criticised for its inappropriate proportions. When the partially built tower collapsed in 1878, killing some ten workers, it caused a national scandal and the Italians were immediately taken off the project. As Ramalho Ortigão so caustically stated at the time, the tower, 'unable to collapse from old age, collapsed from shame'.

The 'restored' Jerónimos Abbey has the air of a piece of stage scenery, conforming to the practices and ideology of the time. A monotonous regularity was imposed on the dormitory building and the Renaissance church porch was lost forever. The even more beautiful Kings' Room (Sala dos Reis), a classical construction whose austerity was regarded as inauthentic, anti-medieval, anti-Manueline and anti-Romantic, was also demolished. Rafael Cardoso and Raimundo Valadas succeeded the Italians but in 1894 work was cut short again. In 1886 the chapter house had been completed to a design by Valadas, with ornamentation by Simões de Almeida, who designed the tomb of the great historian Alexandre Herculano (also president of the then Council of Belém) who had died in 1877. Controversy over the completion of the monastery finally came to an end when, in the first decade of the twentieth century, a plan drawn up by Parente da Silva led to work that finally completed the ruined main block.

The efforts of the set designers and their successors remain a living testimony to an erroneous interpretation of the Manueline style. The shell, anchor and sailing ship motifs adorning the doorposts and fanlights in the dormitories pass – or at least passed at one time – for 'originals'. This forced the 'Manueline' – or as the poet and essayist Guerra Junqueiro ironically dubbed it, 'sub-Manueline' – to be forever linked to the famous maritime symbolism.

It was no accident that Jerónimos Abbey became a great patriotic monument. The nautical symbolism that was seen as representative of the Manueline style automatically became associated with a celebration of Portugal's poets and thinkers. The monument was seen as a memorial to the great discoverers, and fulfilled, to a certain degree, the role for which it was originally built. Beneath the choir of the church lies the tomb of the poet Luís de Camões, beside the sarcophagus of Vasco da Gama. Alexandre Herculano, the great champion of social reform and exponent of Portuguese Romanticism, is also buried in the chapter house. When, in 1940, the impressive World Exhibition was held here, it was staged right in front of the monastery. Salazar also chose the monument as the magnificent backdrop for celebrations of his dictatorship. Finally, in 1985, the remains of the poet Fernando Pessoa were transferred to the cloister, as if in response to the words of his mythical cycle of poems *Mensagem* (*Message*) – a cathartic synthesis of the religious history of Portugal.

THE FAÇADE

The monastery's south façade runs parallel to the river, facing the waterfront. It can be divided into four main sections from left to right. First is the large former dormitory and the arcades beneath, which have undergone successive restorations, then the body of the church itself with its massive aisles. Tall windows and the imposing south portal are cut into its façade. The transept looks on the outside like a box with chamfered edges. A simple rectangular structure with an oculus projects from the transept, corresponding to the south arm. Next is the Mannerist chancel, which, unlike the other sections, has no external decoration. The cupola on the church tower, as mentioned, dates from the nineteenth century.

In terms of composition, the south portal of Jerónimos Abbey is one of Portugal's finest examples of late-Gothic architecture. It was master builder João de Castilho who was responsible for the final design of what he called the 'side door'. The work on this part of the monastery began in 1516 and took more than a year to complete.

Aerial view of
Jerónimos Abbey

THE SOUTH PORTAL

The central position on the south portal of the monastery at Belém is occupied by an image of the Virgin Mary and the infant Jesus. In the Virgin's hand is the vessel containing the gifts from the Three Wise Men. This alludes to Our Lady of the Three Kings, from the time of the monastery's foundation, and references the story of the site's association with Bethlehem and the journeys to the east undertaken by the Portuguese voyagers.

The tympanums show scenes from the life of St Jerome. The saint is depicted removing the thorn from the lion's paw, wearing the vestments of a cardinal, and as a hermit in the desert. Over the tympanum is the Portuguese coat of arms. The figurine at the apex of the entrance arch is St Sebastian and the images on the panel above are of female saints in baldachins.

South portal

Group of Apostles on the east side of the south portal

Statue of Henry the Navigator on the trumeau of the south portal

Plan showing configuration of iconography on the south portal

1 Our Lady of the Three Kings
2 Henry the Navigator
3 The Archangel Michael
4 Portuguese Coat of Arms
5-6 Scenes from the life of
   St Jerome
7 St Jerome
8 St Augustin
9 St Gregory the Great
10 St Ambrose
11 St Catherine
12 St Apollonia
13 St Anastasia
14 St Lucy
15 The Prophet Daniel
16 The Prophet Ezekiel
17 The Prophet Jeremiah
18 The Prophet Isaiah
19 The Apostle Peter
20 The Apostle Paul
21-30 Apostles
31-36 Angels with instruments
37 St Sebastian
38 Medallion (Queen Maria?)
39 Medallion (King Manuel?)
40 Two lions' heads

These figures are interpreted by some to be the Four Sibyls – St Catherine, St Apollonia, St Anastasia and St Lucy. On either side are images of the Prophets – Daniel, Ezekiel, Jeremiah and Isaiah – who foretold the coming of Christ. The upper part consists of the Doctors and Fathers of the Church, with St Jerome and St Augustine on the left, and St Gregory the Great and St Ambrose on the right. The large window is surrounded by an array of angels playing musical instruments. On the lower level are the Twelve Apostles, corresponding to the door jambs of the buttresses.

The array of figures depicted on the portal therefore corresponds with the Testaments Some, such as the Prophets, come from the Old Testament, and others, like the Apostles and the Virgin Mary, from the New Testament. Standing at the top of the portal, in the centre, is the figure of the Archangel Michael, while at the base, against the trumeau, is the image of Prince Henry, with the Virgin and Child between them. Portrayed in this way, St Michael can be seen to occupy the position of mediator, a figure providing the connection between the temporal and celestial worlds. King Manuel was particularly devoted to St Michael and chose him as 'guardian angel of the kingdom' in 1504. It is thought that this was probably as a consequence of the grief he suffered over the death of Prince Miguel two years earlier. The statue of Prince Henry commemorates the monarch's ancestor (he was King Manuel's uncle), who also founded the chapel that predated the monastery. He also represents a link with the House of Avis, as the king came from a side branch of this dynasty and was very much concerned with legitimising his power and his lineage.

Figure of Our Lady of the Three
Kings or Santa Maria de Belém,
on the south portal

Sculpted figures of female saints
and martyrs on the buttress of
the south portal

THE WEST PORTAL

One of the most unusual features of the monastery complex was the long arcade that ran from east to west for nearly 200 metres. According to various early representations of Jerónimos prior to the nineteenth-century restorations, it was an open arcade. It would have been completed by 1516 and the arches closed off later in a somewhat rough-and-ready manner. Nevertheless, in its initial design it would have provided access for people and carriages at any point along its length and been used as a thoroughfare. Above it was a large roofed structure, with windows at more or less regular intervals, which was later converted into a dormitory. It was certainly an unusual building and its purpose is not certain; the chronicles mention that King Manuel wanted these arcades to be used as a kind of warehouse where goods from India could be landed and where business could be contracted. This never happened, and the ground floor was later enclosed and used by the monks for utilitarian purposes, with the remainder leased to tenants outside the monastery.

The iconography of the west portal reinforces the themes depicted on the south portal but here they are more canonical in terms of the theological aspects of Christian mythology in relation to Belém and Bethlehem. At the top of the arch are three

Nativity scene above the door on the west portal

View of the west portal
(Nicolau Chanterêne, 1517)

niches containing sculptures relating to the birth of the Messiah, the Mysteries of the Incarnation of Christ, the Nativity and the Adoration of the Magi. The scene depicting the stable in Bethlehem is in a central position at the top. Statues of the royal founders, accompanied by their respective patron saints, mark the entrance: King Manuel with St Jerome, and his second wife Queen Maria with St John the Baptist. They are presented in both their public capacity and as worshippers, and take the form of lifelike portraits in the tradition of royal mausoleumsy. Here, the positioning of the king and queen mirrors that of the small figures of Joseph and Mary kneeling before the infant Jesus in the central niche above the door, in another reference to the church's patron saint.

However, a different artistic language was used to create the west portal. Nicolau Chanterêne, who was commissioned to undertake the work on 2 January 1517, introduced a classical vocabulary, and the statues he and his artisans produced are distinctly Renaissance in style.

Statue of Queen Maria
on the west portal

Statue of King Manuel and
St Jerome on the west portal

THE CHURCH

The church at Belém is truly monumental. Designed as a hall-church, it has six free-standing pillars – three for each aisle – and two more set further back, forming part of the structure of the upper choir. The pillars are lavishly decorated with Plateresque motifs of grotesques, in a concession to the classical 'Iberian' style associated with João de Castilho's work on the monastery.

The structure of the ceiling, never before seen in Portugal, is a complex net of ribs. The vaulting does not form the usual florid star shapes, instead a net is formed which springs from each pillar in 'palm-tree' bundles extending into tiercerons (intermediate ribs) and liernes (non-structural short ribs) to form eight-point intersections. A further innovation lies in the alternating profile of the transverse arches as the vault

The interior of the church, seen from below the upper choir

passes from the choir to the transept. In turn, the arch above the central nave is semicircular, while those of the side aisles are pointed.

The vaulting over the transept, probably completed in 1522, is equally ambitious. Its profile is slightly depressed, with the two transverse arches joining the piers to the east wall being the most significant and defining element of the construction. This system divides the vault into six sections inside which ribs create a four-pointed star with a central diamond shape, joined in the middle by a boss. Seven of these bosses are surrounded by circular curved ribs, which add to the overall flattened appearance of the ceiling. The design enables the side aisles and central nave to form a unified space for the congregation. The idea was to provide space for a vast assembly of people

The interior of the church, seen from halfway up the chancel

to gather in the great hall of the nave during religious services.

The church was also designed as a setting for an opulent display of regal power; the dimensions and content of the iconography would have been governed by the need to eulogise and glorify the monarch.

The ways in which the king was exalted in public oratory and in the exaggerated accounts of great royal feats can be seen in fictionalised chronicles such as João de Barros's *Crónica do Imperador Clarimundo* (c. 1520) or the prologue and the narrative of the *Crónica de D. Afonso Henriques* by Duarte Galvão (written before 1517). Both highlight the association of national destiny with the Miracle of Ourique, which sanctified the Portuguese coat of arms. On the eve of the battle of Ourique (1139), King Afonso Henrique saw a vision of the Crucifixion. In the ensuing battle he defeated five Moorish kings and adopted their five shields as his coat of arms, incorporating the five wounds of Christ to commemorate the miraculous encounter. These examples show that inscriptions such as *In Hoc Signo Vinces* (In This Sign Conquer), which was the motto of the first Christian Roman Emperor Constantine, which appear next to the Crucifixion in the chancel of the church of Santa Cruz in Coimbra or on the coins issued by the king, are based on a well-founded 'myth of origins'.

In this way the iconography used in the church was chosen to pay homage to the king. It was never completed, however, and some 130 niches incorporated into the architectural supports remain empty of sculptures. Their exact purpose remains a mystery, although Rafael Moreira has suggested that the niches were 'perhaps intended to hold protective effigies of the Portuguese royal family, the seventeen rulers beginning with Henry of Burgundy, or their patron saints. The display here of an "ancestors' gallery" and their insignias would be a clear proclamation of the sacred and providential nature of the royal lineage'. To support this hypothesis Moreira cites the examples of San Juan de Los Reyes in Toledo, the tomb of Emperor Maximilian in Innsbruck, Westminster Abbey and the Chapel of King's College, Cambridge. These and other arguments suggest that the church was intended as a national monument, where a procession of monarchs might keep a watchful eye over political and diplomatic business.

In addition to speculations about the secular imagery there are various theories relating to the sacred images. The Twelve Apostles above the twelve confessionals and the Four Evangelists in the niches above the transept are arranged in a logical sequence. The remaining niches are similarly occupied but in no obvious order. It is possible that, with some of them filled, logic broke down in the interests of getting the job done. According to Rafael Moreira the transept 'was not a space for processions but a meeting point and hence a holy place in which rituals of state were performed, deliberately designed to serve as a backdrop to the various acts involving the monarch in his role as mediator between the life of the nation and the realm of the divine; from liturgical celebrations to civic functions and funerals'.

If we accept this quite reasonable view we might assume that the medallion showing a figure in profile and executed with the precision of a portrait, interpreted variously as the master builder in charge of the project – either Boitaca or João de Castilho – should in fact be considered to be a portrait of King Manuel. The portrait has

the monarch's characteristic features and occupies a privileged position within the church – on the pillar on the north side and facing the chancel – close to the place where, as specified in his will, he was to be buried. Although only contracted to complete the church in 1522 it is likely that João de Castilho would have taken account of the monarch's wishes.

At the other end, the choir of the church (one of the first high choirs in either Portugal or Spain) is an architectural construction from a slightly later date than the rest of the church, one which was fitted into pre-existing structures. It too was restored following the earthquake of 1755. On the ground floor or lower choir, next to the west door, are two chapels: the Chapel of St Leonard on the right as you go in, and the Chapel of the Way of the Cross on the left. In 1940 the tombs of Vasco da Gama and Luís de Camões were moved into the lower choir. Both were sculpted in 1894 by Costa Mota Tio in a reproduction, neo-Manueline style very much in keeping with the aesthetics of the nineteenth-century restorations of the building. The presence of these two leading figures transformed the church into a patriotic shrine and a symbolic, albeit unofficial, national pantheon. The remarkable choir stalls are the highlight of the upper choir. This U-shaped group is one of the most outstanding works of Renaissance carving in Portugal. Designed without doubt by Diogo de Torralva, it was built around 1550 by Spanish woodcarver Diego de Zarza, possibly in collaboration with the Flemish woodcarver Philippe de Vries. Its structure today consists of sixty stalls arranged in two rows, upper and lower. The seats, with their misericords and their exceptionally high backs, are built of chestnut or Flanders oak. There were originally eighty-four stalls, before a part of the side elevations was dismantled and removed. The lower row is decorated with secular motifs – ships, festivities, satyrs – interspersed with small figures of Atlas or fantastical motifs of clearly Flemish inspiration. On the upper row, busts in the 'classical' style alternate with figures of saints.

The choir has an extraordinary dignity. The quality of the craftsmanship in the woodcarving, in which the architectural principle of the projecting pilasters combines with the vocabulary of the High Renaissance, ranks alongside the work of the finest artists in Europe. On the choir balustrade, which was restored in the nineteenth century, is a monumental image of Christ on the Cross, given to the monastery by Prince Luís, King Manuel's son, in 1551. It was a particular favourite of King Philip I of Spain who was impressed by its dramatic realism. This uniquely expressive image was also a precursor of Mannerism.

The south side of the upper choir, with choir stalls

Detail of choir stall

THE CHANCEL

Detail of the sacrarium door
(João de Sousa, 1674–1678)

Altarpiece in the chancel
(Lourenço de Salzedo, 1570–1572)

The present chancel was commissioned by Queen Catarina, who acted as regent for the infant King Sebastian from 1557 to 1562. The political situation in Portugal led Catarina to assume a decisive role in affairs of state and her increased status was reflected in a more assertive style of architecture. Jerónimo de Ruão, who drew up the plans, was inspired by aesthetic principles that were highly innovative in their classicism, while following principles of interpretation that can only be described as Mannerist. The first section of the chancel has a rectangular floor plan, the second is semicircular. The far wall continues up into the roof and there are deep-set windows in the side walls. The grid formed by the mouldings on the far wall frame the panels of the altarpiece. There were originally six of these panels but only five remain.

Between the columns of the side walls are the arcosolia (vaulted stone chambers) containing the tombs of King Manuel and Queen Maria on the Gospel (or right) side, and King João III and Queen Catarina on the Epistle (or left) side. The tombs have a classical pyramidal shape and are supported by two marble elephants clearly inspired by the mausoleums of the Malatesta Temple in Rimini, Italy. The tombs bear Latin inscriptions by the humanist André de Resende. This style of architecture, of which one of the most avant-garde features is the contrasting use of white, blue and pink marble from the Alentejo region, was much admired by Philip II of Spain, who commissioned the design. The outlines of the tombs, and the way in which the sculptor defines volume and surface, produce a curious sense that space itself is being modelled, something that can only be compared with the small-scale 'architecture' produced by other craftsmen such as goldsmiths and silversmiths. The iconography of the chancel is

highly austere and it is the architecture itself that predominates, both in the use of the Classical Orders and in the perfection of its proportions. This innovative arrangement draws the eye irresistibly to the dramatic, brightly coloured retable behind the altar.

The retable, by Lourenço de Salzedo (1535–78), was completed between 1570 and 1572. According to the art historian Vítor Serrão it is one of the most impressive and earliest manifestations of Portuguese Mannerist painting in its mature, classical phase. The retable is divided into two rows. The upper row consists of three panels depicting scenes from Christ's Passion: in the centre is the Deposition, flanked by Jesus carrying the Cross and Jesus bound to the pillar. The lower row has two panels (formerly three) with scenes from the Nativity and the Adoration of the Magi. The missing panel from the centre showed the Madonna and Child. The decorative scheme of the chancel, although completed over sixty years after the monastery was founded, still centred on themes relating to the patron saint of the church.

The iconography, use of colour and the shape of the figures reveal Salzedo to have been attuned to contemporary trends in art. His work illustrates the influence of the Italian school and he produced work of the same *terribilità* (intense emotional power) as Michelangelo, in complete contrast to the meek ceremoniousness of official high art. The acid colours and the elongated composition of the figures add a monu-mental grandeur to the altarpiece, rein-forcing its didactic message and capturing the prevailing mood of the Catholic Church in the early years of the Counter Reformation, following the Council of Trent. In the centre stands a majestic Baroque sacrarium made by goldsmith João de

Sousa between 1674 and 1678. The central panel of the Mannerist retable was removed to make way for this piece.

Because of the importance of Jerónimos Abbey as one of Portugal's architectural and artistic showcases, it came to house some of the finest examples of late Gothic, Portuguese Renaissance and Mannerist art. Paradoxically it also served as a springboard for establishing the language and forms of the late classical revival, marking the end of an era in the nation's history. With the death of King Sebastião the Avis-Beja dynasty came to an end and so too did the golden age of discovery. Work at Belém also came to a standstill.

A curious phenomenon is said to occur at the monastery at certain times of the year, when the sun's rays enter the church in a particular way. It may be purely coincidental, although it is conceivable that the alignment of the dormitory, the rose window (originally a large rectangular window) and the body of the church was deliberate. The event was reported by the chronicler Father Diogo de Jesus and corroborated by Father Jacinto de S. Miguel. It was described by Father Felicidade Alves, a former parish priest of the monastery, that for twenty days before the spring equinox and between 28 October and the thirtieth day after the autumn equinox 'the sun's golden rays... from the hour of evensong until sunset, entering from the west and covering a distance of 450 paces, pass in a straight line through the whole space of the dormitory, choir and church to the sacrarium, reflecting on the floor as though a goldsmith had gilded it with fire. It seems as though the sun were asking its Creator for leave of absence from such an illustrious monastery for the brief hours of the night, promising to return again to shine at dawn'.

The chancel
(Jerónimo de Ruão, 1565?–1572)

THE SACRISTY

Although hidden away in a discreet corner of the monastery at the side of the transept, the sacristy is a small architectural jewel with a square floor plan and, at the top, an innovative central pillar from which ribs fan out to support the depressed vault. The configuration of the vaulting, with its curved circular ribs resting on the twisted corbels of the engaged columns, is very much like the fan vaulting found in Great Britain.

A sober arcade runs along the walls. Its uncluttered and well-proportioned design is attributed to Jerónimo de Ruão. On the back wall are fourteen paintings describing the life of St Jerome, attributed to Simão Rodrigues and dating from between 1600 and 1610. The remaining paintings displayed here probably come from other parts of the monastery. They include a series of six panels by António Campelo showing scenes from Christ's Passion, presumably the paintings that formerly occupied the large niches in the cloister.

The sacristy

THE CLOISTER
AND MANUELINE
IMPERIAL RHETORIC

The entrance to the cloister was once the main point of entry to the monastery, a door set slightly back in the recess between the west façade of the church and the dormitory building. It is a classicist architectural composition designed by Teodósio de Frias in 1625 and executed by the stonemason Diogo Vaz. Two large busts of Hercules and Julius Caesar stand on either side of the door, framing a tablet bearing a Latin inscription by André de Resende which reads: 'Vasta mole sacrum divinae in littore matri / Rex posuit regus maximum Emmanuel. / Auxit opus heres rfegni, et pietatis, uterque / Structura certant, religione pares', which translates as 'King Manuel, the greatest of kings, built on the waterfront / a vast and magnificent church, dedicated to the Mother of God. / The heir to his kingdom and his piety continued his work. / Equal in faith, each seeks to surpass the other in this construction'.

The structure of the enclosure is unusual and nothing of its kind had been seen before. The ground plan is square, with the corners cut off to form what is virtually an octagon. The decision to build two storeys entirely out of stone was a major innovation. The various stages of its construction are not immediately obvious, particularly on the ground floor, but a closer inspection reveals that the original design envisaged a simpler decorative scheme. The cloister was designed by Boitaca and includes many features characteristic of his late-Gothic style, including cylindrical external pilasters and buttresses. Work on the cloister would still have been in progress when João de Castilho took over, with the walls partially completed but probably without their vaults, or at least with only those of the east and west sides completed. Aware of the complex ornamental and iconographic scheme that

Entrance hall of the monastery, leading to the cloister

was demanded, Castilho updated the original plan by adding to the structure. He also covered Boitaca's original cylindrical pilasters with rectangular ones, decorating them with Plateresque-style reliefs. Some of the original pilasters and buttresses can, however, still be seen on the upper storey, giving us an idea of Boitaca's original design for the cloister.

However, the overall atmosphere that reigns in the cloister, with its eclectic and opulent ornamentation, is distinctly Manueline. Almost all the decoration in the arcades consists of plant motifs, with some animal images and fantasy figures combining to produce an exotic, magical atmosphere. The unexpected combination of late-Gothic animal, plant and allegorical motifs with a more learned and contemporary Lombard style of ornamentation resulted in a uniquely creative architectural and artistic composition. The rich decorative and ornamental scheme alone bears the stamp of a new aesthetic approach that is testimony to the building's stylistic primacy.

Indeed the cloister shows evidence of a didactic purpose in its intertwining of Christian and royal symbolism. The Christian themes that appear are related to the *devotio moderna* (new devotion) so dear to 'old queen' Leonor, King Manuel's sister, and to the Jeronimite monks themselves, who were responsible for the spiritual renewal of Portuguese monasticism. The adoption of the life of Christ as a model for emulation, reflected in the widespread influence of books such as the *Vita Christi*, written by the Carthusian monk Ludolph of Saxony, or the *Boosco Deleitoso*, a moral allegory based on the life of an ascetic hermit, turned Christ's Passion into an ethical, moral and religious touchstone and formed a new spirituality centred on the figure of Christ.

Allegory of Charity

The cloister (Diogo Boitaca, 1502–1513; João de Castilho, 1517–c.1520)

Relief in the south-east corner of the cloister: the Portuguese coat of arms supported by dragons

The symbolism inherent in the cloister should be read with this in mind, particularly with regards to the set of medallions representing the Instruments of the Passion of Christ, in what is the most complete decorative scheme of its kind in Portugal. Here, the presentation of the Instruments in tablets and shields fulfils their traditional role as 'Christ's coat of arms'. There are ten in total, distributed around the four galleries, but mainly on the east and west corridors. Seen as an expression of the Passion itself, through a journey which is both a physical and symbolic pilgrimage, they embody the search for the *via unitiva* – the mystical union with Christ through prayer. Images like the Instruments of the Passion and other Christian symbols such as the globe, IHS (the monogram for the name of Jesus in Greek, first used by the Franciscans), the Cross and the Five Wounds of Christ define the cloister as a place of contemplation.

Relief in the north-east corner of the cloister: The Annunciation

Relief of the Crown of Thorns

While the dominant symbolism on the east and west sides is religious, that on the north and south façades is more secular. On the north side are tablets bearing symbols of the monarchy: the armillary sphere (the emblem of King Manuel) and the bunch of white lilies (emblem of his second wife Queen Maria). Next to them are essentially Christian symbols: the IHS, the crowned 'M' (which may refer to Manuel, Queen Maria or the Virgin Mary) and the Five Wounds. The wing ends with a relief depicting the Annunciation. On the south façade is the coat of arms of Avis in relief, followed by four medallions containing images thought by some to represent the Portuguese navigators Pedro Álvares Cabral, Nicolau Coelho, Vasco da Gama and Paulo da Gama. However, they have also been interpreted as four nobles of Antiquity – great emperors or generals often cited in texts extolling imperialistic virtues. Beyond them is a representation of the sun and, in the corners, the coats of arms of the king and queen of Portugal, which seem to mark the physical and human boundaries of their empire.

The imagery may be viewed as an expression of the mythical connection between Jesus (Emmanuel) and the king, and between the Virgin Mary and Queen Maria. It is clear that King Manuel believed that his name shaped his destiny. It was the same name as the infant Emmanuel who Isaiah prophesied (Isaiah 7: 10-14) would be born of a virgin, a sign that Jerusalem would be set free – the prophecy that St Matthew interpreted as predicting the birth of Jesus (Matthew 1: 23). Contemporary chroniclers and the writers of royal eulogies made much of this comparison, associating it with the divine right of kings, a frequent topic in their writings.

If we interpret the imagery on the north side of the cloister as representing the 'Christian cycle', focusing on Jesus and Mary and the divinity of the monarch, then the south side can be seen as the 'heroic cycle', devoted to human and national exploits. If we then consider the parallels between the two iconographies, we see that here is a representation of the intersection of the history of Portugal and the known world with the history of Christianity. The monarch assumes a role as intermediary, both apostolic and heroic. Christianity and its traditions are in themselves the most powerful expression of the glory of the empire and its ruler, King Manuel.

The images in baldachins on the upper storey, on the veranda of the cloister, complement those on the lower storey. The most striking aspect of the whole iconographic scheme is the powerful presence of the cardinal, theological and common virtues: Faith, Charity and Prudence on the west side, together with the allegorical figure of the Church; Fortitude, Liberality and Temperance on the north side; and Hope and Justice on the east, accompanied by King Manuel and the figure of the Prophet Isaiah. It comes as no surprise to find the monarch in the company of the Prophet Isaiah and the figure of Hope, both of which had personal resonance for him. He regarded his name as a direct reference to Isaiah's prophecy, while his emblem – the armillary sphere – was interpreted by contemporary chroniclers and heralds as a visual pun: *sphera do mundo* (the earth's sphere) and the *spera mundi* (the hope of the world).

The imagery used at Jerónimos Abbey can be understood as part of a practical culture based on the rules of rhetoric and the use of mnemonics to deliver a message that was particularly relevant in King Manuel's time. At the same time it brought together a compendium of worldly knowledge and divine and regal power. It also intensified the effects of a form of architecture that epitomised grandeur and that was designed to proclaim the might of both the sovereign and his God.

The rich symbolism of the decorations in the cloister of Jerónimos Abbey, and of the south portal, has engendered a series of esoteric interpretations, among them the fascinating speculations to be found in the scholarly and compelling writings of the mysterious twentieth-century alchemist Fulcanelli, who claimed that the secrets of alchemy were openly displayed on the walls of Gothic cathedrals. Another outstanding contribution to the debate comes from António Telmo, with his intelligent and inspiring interpretation of the stones of the cloister, in which he sees the history of Portugal and its destiny prophetically inscribed. We should exercise caution, however, when considering these extra

dimensions, and focus on what is actually known, except to acknowledge the curious and poetic magic that the monastery possesses. The experience of visiting Jerónimos Abbey can be further enhanced by reading its messages in conjunction with *Mensagem (Message)*, the enigmatic volume of poems by Fernando Pessoa, who was photographed here.

Medallion in the south gallery:
the sun with twelve rays or
Sol Justitiae

The armillary sphere, emblem of King Manuel, with the royal crown. The inscription reads: I.EMANVEL R.P. ET ALG. V. (Manuel I King of Portugal and the Algarves)

Tomb of Luís de Camões
(Costa Mota Tio, 1894)

Tomb of Vasco da Gama
(Costa Mota Tio, 1894)

The church, with the ceiling
above the transept crossing
in the foreground

BIBLIOGRAPHY

ALVES, Ana Maria, *Iconologia do Poder Real no Período Manuelino*, Lisbon, I.N.-C M., 1985.

ALVES, José da Felicidade, *O Mosteiro dos Jerónimos*, vol. I, Lisbon, Horizonte, 1989.

ATANAZIO, M. C. Mendes, *A Arte do Manuelino*, Lisbon, Presença, 1984.

AVERINI, Ricardo, 'Sul Manuelino' in *Colóquio Artes*, 2nd series, nº 56, Mar. 1983.

BARREIRA, João, *Arte portuguesa. Evolução estética*, Lisbon, Exselsior, undated.

BARROS, João de, *Décadas da Ásia*, I, Coimbra, 1932.

BARROS, João de, *Panegíricos*, Lisbon, Sá da Costa, 2nd ed., 1943.

BARROS, João de, *Crónica do Imperador Clarimundo*, 2 vols., Lisbon, Sá da Costa, 1953.

Boosco Deleitoso, (1515 edition of text: introduction, notes and glossary by Augusto Magne), Rio de Janeiro, Ministério da Educação e Saúde / Instituto Nacional do Livro, 1950.

BRANDI, Cesare, 'Il Manuelino' in *Struttura e Architettura*, Turin, Einaudi, 2nd ed. 1971, pp.301-307.

CHICÓ, Mario Tavares, 'A arquitectura em Portugal na época de D. Manuel e nos princípios do reinado de D. João III. O gótico final português, o estilo manuelino e a introdução da arte do renascimento' in *História da Arte em Portugal* (ed. Aarão de Lacerda), vol. II, Oporto, Portucalense Editora, 1948, pp.225-324.

CORREIA, Vergílio, *As obras de Santa Maria de Belém 1514 a 1519*, Lisbon, 1922.

CORREIA, Vergílio, *Monumentos e Esculturas*, Lisbon, 1924.

CORREIA, Vergílio, *A Arquitectura em Portugal no séc. XVI*, Sep. 'Biblos', vol. V, 1-2, Coimbra, Universidade de Coimbra, 1929.

CORREIA, Vergílio, 'Arte: ciclo manuelino' in *História de Portugal* (Barcelos), vol. IV, Portucalense Editora, 1933, pp.433-474.

DESWARTE, Sylvie, *Les Enluminures de la 'Leitura Nova' 1504-1522*, Paris, Fondation Calouste Gulbenkian, 1977.

DIAS, Pedro, 'A Arquitectura do Gótico final e a decoração Manuelina' in *O Manuelino* (vol. 5, da História de Arte em Portugal), Lisbon, Publicações Alfa, 1986, pp. 7-91.

DIAS, Pedro, *A Arquitectura Manuelina*, Oporto, 1988.

DIAS, Pedro, *Os Portais Manuelinos do Mosteiro dos Jerónimos*, Coimbra, Universidade de Coimbra, 1993.

EVIN, Paul A., *Étude sur le style manuélin*, Paris, 1948.

Bust in relief
(possibly Vasco da Gama)

Bust in relief
(possibly Pedro Álvares Cabral)

The north façade
of the cloister

EVIN, Paul A., 'Style manuelin et Spatgotik: les critiques du symbolisme maritime' in *Ciência e Trópico*, No 2, vol. 13, 1985.

EVIN, Paul A., 'Faut-il voir un symbolisme maritime dans la décoration Manueline?' in *Acte du Congrés International d'Histoire de l'Arte*, vol. 2, 1949, pp.191-198.

FRANCO, Anísio (ed.), *Jerónimos. 4 Séculos de Pintura*, exhibition catalogue, Lisbon, IPPC, 1992.

GOIS, Damião de, *Crónica do Felicíssimo Rei D. Manuel*, 4 vols., Coimbra, Imp. da Univ., 1949-54.

GOIS, Damião de, *Descrição da Cde de Lisboa*, Lisbon, Horizonte, 1988.

KUBLER, Georges, *Portuguese Plain Architecture*, Middletown Wesleyan University Press, undated.

LACERDA, Aarão de (dir.), *História da Arte em Portugal*, vol. I, Oporto, 1942.

LAMBERT, Élie, 'L'Art Manuelin' in *XVI Congres d'Histoire de l'Art.*, vol. I, Lisbon - Oporto, 1949, pp.13-20.

LEITE, Ana Cristina, PEREIRA, Paulo, 'Para uma leitura da simbólica manuelina, in *Prelo*, No 5, Out. - Dez. - 1984, pp.51-74.

LEITE, Ana Cristina, PEREIRA, Paulo, 'São João verde, o Selvagem e o Gigante em Gil Vicente - apontamento iconológico' in *Estudos Portugueses. Homenagem a Luciana Stegagno Picchio*, Lisbon, Difel, 1991.

MARIAS, Fernando, *El Largo Siglo XVI*, Madrid, Taurus, 1989.

MARKL, Dagoberto, BAPTISTA PEREIRA, Fernando António, *O Renascimento*, vol.6 da *História da Arte em Portugal*. Lisbon, Publicações Alfa, 1986.

MIGUEL, Fr. Jacinto de S., *Mosteiro de Belém*, Lisbon, 1901.

MOREIRA, Rafael, 'Arquitectura' in *Catalogue of the 17th Exhibition of Art, Science and Culture of the Council of Europe, Arte Antiga - I*, Lisbon, 1983, pp. 307-352.

MOREIRA, Rafael, *Jerónimos*, Lisbon, Verbo, 1987.

MOREIRA, Rafael, *A Arquitectura do Renascimento no Sul de Portugal*, Lisbon, 1991.

MOREIRA, Rafael, *A Arquitectura Militar na Expansão Portuguesa*, Oporto, CNCDP, 1994a.

MOREIRA, Rafael, 'Santa Maria de Belém' in *O Livro de Lisboa*, Lisbon, Lisboa 94 / Horizonte, 1994.

MOREIRA, Rafael, 'A Torre de Belém' in *O Livro de Lisboa*, Lisbon, Lisboa 94 / Horizonte, 1994.

MUCHAGATO, Jorge, SAPIEHA, Nicolas, Jerónimos. Memória e Lugar do Real Mosteiro, Lisbon, Inapa, 1997.

PAIS DA SILVA, J. H, 'Rotas Artísticas no Reinado de D. Manuel I', *Panorama*, 4th series, 32, 1969.

PAIS DA SILVA, J. H, 'Manuelino' in *Enciclopédia Luso - Brasileira de Cultura*, vol. 12, Lisbon, ed. Verbo, 1971.

PEREIRA, Paulo, LEITE, Ana Cristina, 'Espiritualidade e religiosidade na Lisboa de Quinhentos' in *Lisboa Quinhentista*. Exhibition

Upper storey of the cloister

Catalogue, Lisbon, Câmara Municipal de Lisboa, 1983, pp.31-41.

PEREIRA, Paulo, *A Obra Silvestre e a Esfera do Rei*, Coimbra, Universidade de Coimbra, 1990.

PEREIRA, Paulo, 'L'architecture portugaise (1400-1550)' in *Feitorias*, exhibition catalogue (curator Pedro Dias), Antuérpia, Europália 91, 1991.

PEREIRA, Paulo, 'Retórica e Memória na simbologia manuelina. O caso de Santa Maria de Belém', Lisbon, *Jerónimos. 4 Séculos de Pintura* (dir. Anísio Franco), exhibition catalogue, Lisbon, IPPC, 1992a.

PEREIRA, Paulo, 'Gil Vicente e a contaminação das artes' in *Temas Vicentinos. Actas do Colóquio em torno da obra de Gil Vicente*, Lisbon, Diálogo, 1992.

PEREIRA, Paulo, 'A conjuntura artística e as mudanças de gosto' in *História de Portugal* (ed. José Mattoso), vol. III (ed. J.R.Magalhães), Lisbon, Círculo de Leitores, 1993.

PEREIRA, Paulo, 'Architecture manuéline: thèmes et problèmes de méthode' in *A Travers L'Image*, Paris, Klinksieck / CNRS, 1993a.

PEREIRA, Paulo, *Lisboa Manuelina*, Lisbon, IPM, 1994.

PEREIRA, Paulo, 'Iconografia dos Descobrimentos' in *Dicionário de História dos Descobrimentos*, vol. I, Lisbon, Círculo de Leitores, 1994.

QUADROS, António, *Introdução a uma estética existencial*, Lisbon, 1954.

QUINET, Edgar, *Mes vacances en Espagne*, Paris, Hachette, 1954.

SANSONETTI, Paul - Georges, 'Da Távola Redonda à Esfera Armilar: Ideal cavaleiresco e domínio do Mundo' in *Cavalaria Espiritual e Conquista do Mundo*, Lisbon, I.N.I.C., 1986, pp.43-48.

SANTOS, Cândido dos, *Os monges de S. Jerónimo em Portugal na Época do Renascimento*, I.C.L.P., Biblioteca Breve, 1984.

SANTOS, Reinaldo dos, *A Torre de Belém*, Coimbra, Imp. da Univ., 1922.

SANTOS, Reinaldo dos, 'O Mosteiro de Belém' in *A Arte em Portugal*, No 10, Oporto, Marques Abreu, 1930.

SANTOS, Reinaldo dos, 'O Estilo Manuelino' in *Boletim da Academia Nacional de Belas Artes*, 1947.

SANTOS, Reinaldo dos, *O Estilo Manuelino*, Lisbon, 1952.

SANTOS, Reinaldo dos, *Oito séculos de Arte Portuguesa*, Lisbon, undated .

SOUSA, Abade de Castro e, *Descripção do Real Mosteiro de Belém*, Lisbon, 2nd ed., 1840.

TELMO, António, *História Secreta de Portugal*, Lisbon, Guimarães, 1977.

TORRES, Fr. Alvaro de Torres, *Dialogo espiritual* (intro. Candido dos Santos), Oporto, 1974.

VASCONCELOS, Joaquim de, *Da Architectura Manuelina*, Coimbra, 1885.

VIEIRA DA SILVA, José Custódio, *O tardo-gótico na arquitectura. A arquitectura religiosa do Alto Alentejo*, Lisbon, Horizonte, 1989.

VIEIRA DA SILVA, José Custódio, *Paço Medievais Portugueses. Caracterização e Evolução da Habitação Nobre. Séculos XII a XVI*, Lisbon, 1995.